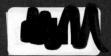

DO NOT REMOVE
CARDS FROM POCKET

JENNIFER CAPRIATI

TEENAGE TENNIS STAR

BY BILL GUTMAN

MILLBROOK SPORTS WORLD
THE MILLBROOK PRESS
BROOKFIELD, CONNECTICUT

Published by The Millbrook Press
2 Old New Milford Road
Brookfield, CT 06804

Created in association with Grey Castle Press, Inc.
Series Editorial Director: *Elizabeth Simon*
Art Director: *Nancy Driscoll*
Design Management: *Italiano-Perla Design*

Photographs courtesy of: Russ Adams: cover, 20-21, 25, 28-29,
31, 33, 38-39, 43; John W. McDonough: cover inset, 44;
David Becker: 3, 4, 7; *The Miami Herald:* 8, 11,
12, 18, 46; AP/Wide World Photos: 15, 16, 23, 35.

Library of Congress Cataloging-in-Publication Data

Gutman, Bill.
Jennifer Capriati, teenage tennis star / by Bill Gutman.
p. cm. — (Millbrook sports world)
Includes bibliographical references (p. 46) and index.
Summary: Traces the tennis career of the young American
player who made her professional debut at age thirteen.
ISBN 1-56294-225-5
1. Capriati, Jennifer —Juvenile literature.
2. Tennis players—United States—
Biography—Juvenile literature.
[1. Capriati, Jennifer. 2. Tennis players.] I. Title. II. Series.
GV994.C36G88 1993
796.342'092—dc20
[B]
92-18163 CIP AC

JENNIFER CAPRIATI

It was a searing March afternoon at The Polo Club at Boca Raton. In spite of the heat, tennis fans flocked to the small stadium to watch the first round of the 1990 Virginia Slims of Florida tournament. This was only one tournament on the women's pro tour, and it wasn't an especially important one. But this year there *was* a special attraction.

A young tennis player—not yet 14 years old—was making her professional debut. Jennifer Capriati didn't seem nervous as she walked out onto the court to face Mary Lou Daniels, who once had been ranked 15th in the world and was nearly 15 years her senior.

Jennifer Capriati's first professional tournament made news all around the tennis world. She was not quite 14 years old and went all the way to the finals before losing.

Capriati smiled and waved to the crowd. As she completed her warm-ups her grin disappeared. A look of determination took its place. It was the look of an athlete—an intense competitor who didn't like to lose. Once the match started, it was obvious that Capriati's skills were way beyond her years.

The first set was a series of peaks and valleys. Capriati started out on fire. Hitting a sharp forehand and a blistering, two-fisted backhand, she raced to a 3-0 lead in the first set. She seemed sure and confident, playing mostly from the baseline, but also rushing the net several times. At that point the crowd began rooting for Daniels to make a match of it.

When Daniels picked up her game, Capriati stumbled. She lost six of the next eight games and trailed, 6-5. During the last three games, her shots were all over the place, ending up in the net or out of bounds. Pam Shriver, another veteran pro, thought Capriati was coming apart.

"I panicked for Jennifer," said Shriver, "because I thought it had gotten to her totally. It looked as if it were becoming a nightmare."

But Shriver and most of the others who were watching didn't yet know how tough Jennifer Capriati was. She pulled herself together and tied the set at 6-6 on her next serve. Now it was time for the tiebreaker. The first player who won 7 points would win the game and the set. Capriati simply overwhelmed Daniels, 7-1, and took the set.

This gave her the confidence she needed. In the second set, her accurate ground strokes were too much for Daniels, who began making errors while Capriati's game flowed. She won the set easily, 6-1, to close out the match.

After it ended, photographers and reporters swarmed around the winner. Capriati smiled and hugged her family and friends. Mary Lou Daniels was so

Because she made her pro debut near her home in Florida, Jennifer was a great crowd favorite. Jennifer loved the support and often greeted her fans with smiles and handshakes.

impressed that she compared Capriati with Steffi Graf, then the world's number-one player.

"Steffi hits a heavy ball," Daniels said, "but I'd say Jennifer is right up there with her."

Capriati told the huge gathering that she was "excited" about winning her match. Then the 13-year-old added, "But I think the media is a little out of control."

AN EARLY START

No one can predict where the next great athletes will come from or who they will be. Whenever a toddler picks up a ball, a bat, a glove, or a racket, there is a chance that a great athlete has been born. But more often than not, it's just the act of a curious child. Great athletes are few and far between.

Jennifer Capriati first picked up a tennis racket when she was three. She had been around tennis from the day she was born—and even before that. Her father, Stefano Capriati, was a tennis instructor on Long Island, New York, when his wife, Denise Capriati, was pregnant with Jennifer. Mrs. Capriati took lessons from her husband until the day before her baby was born.

As a nine-year-old in 1985, Jennifer had the quick smile of a happy child. By that time, however, she had already been playing tennis for five years.

"Stefano knew Jennifer would be a tennis player before she was even born just by the way I carried her," Mrs. Capriati has often joked.

Jennifer was born on March 29, 1976. She was the Capriatis's first child. Her brother, Steven, was born several years later. Mr. Capriati says he noticed some unusual qualities in his daughter almost immediately.

"She was always a strong baby," he said. "She liked to crawl behind the ball machine and play with the tennis balls while I taught. I wanted to keep her in the shade, but she always crawled after the balls."

By the time she was four, Jennifer was beginning to hit balls with a small racket. "She could already rally a hundred times on the court," her father said.

It was about that time that the Capriati family moved to Lauderhill, Florida. Their purpose was to put themselves and their daughter into a year-round tennis environment. To some it might seem strange that a family would simply pick up and move like that, but Stefano and Denise Capriati were used to it.

Stefano Capriati had played soccer while growing up in Milan, Italy. When he was in his twenties, he moved to Spain where he also began to play tennis. In Spain he worked as a stuntman in the movies. He was in films such as *Patton*, *The Last Run*, and *100 Rifles*. During this time he met his future wife. Denise, who was born in New York City, eventually became a flight attendant with Pan American Airlines. During a stopover in Spain, she met Stefano.

So the family was used to traveling. As soon as they reached Florida they began to look for a well-known coach. The man they wanted was

Jimmy Evert, Chris Evert's father, one of the greatest players of all time. Mr. Evert was the teaching pro at Holiday Park in Fort Lauderdale.

The Capriatis asked for lessons for their daughter. Mr. Evert looked at little Jennifer and said, "She's too young for me. I don't start teaching kids until they're five."

But Mr. Capriati convinced Evert to watch Jennifer hit the ball. Jimmy Evert was impressed enough to agree to give her a lesson.

"She just struck me right away as having a lot of raw talent," said Mr. Evert. "She was always a bubbly child."

That was the beginning of five years of lessons under Mr. Evert. During that time, Jennifer often hit tennis balls with Chris Evert, who visited her family whenever she could. These were moments Jennifer would never forget.

"The first time I practiced with her I was so nervous I couldn't even keep the ball in the court," Jennifer said. "She probably thought I was really bad."

But Jennifer was far from bad. From the beginning, she was among the best for her age. She enjoyed tennis and practiced all the time—her parents never had to force her. But Mr. and Mrs. Capriati made sure that their daughter's life stayed in balance. School was always a top priority, and Jennifer consistently earned A's.

"I always wanted Jennifer to have as much of a normal life as she could," said Mrs. Capriati. "We didn't want to take her childhood away from her. She loved tennis and was always willing to sacrifice, but she also loved school and her friends."

By the time she was 10 years old, Jennifer was getting so good that it was hard to find competition in Lauderhill. Even her coach knew it was time to move on. "She was beating every player in town, man or woman," said Jimmy Evert.

So the family moved to Wesley Chapel, Florida, to be near Harry Hopman and the Saddlebrook International Tennis Center. Hopman was the long-time coach of the Australian Davis Cup team and one of the best coaches ever. Jennifer began working every day with all the coaches at the Center. Coaching director Tommy Thompson said that Jennifer had so much natural skill that he didn't want to over-coach her.

"She plays on adrenaline and emotion," Thompson said. "You don't want to cloud that with strategy."

On the tennis court, nine-year-old Jennifer hit her strokes hard and with the determination of a champion.

AMATEUR CHAMPION

There was little doubt that Jennifer Capriati had talent. She was winning a slew of amateur tournaments, often beating much older players. Working at Saddlebrook Center, she got even better. Before long, the Capriatis were thinking about the day when she would become a professional. There was little doubt that she would soon be good enough.

"She's just a happy-go-lucky kid," said Rick Macci, one of her coaches, "but put a tennis racket in her hand and she turns killer."

Macci meant that Jennifer hated to lose. "I like to fight," she has said more than once. "When I hear the crowd getting into it, I really get into it too."

When Jennifer was 12, everyone found out just how good she was. That's when she became the youngest girl ever to win both the national 18-and-under clay-court championship and the 18-and-under hard-court title. Not long after that, she won the junior championships at both the French and U.S. Open tournaments. At the age of 12, she was ranked second among all the world's 18-and-under amateurs by the International Tennis Federation.

By this time the family was living in Saddlebrook, Florida, having moved from Wesley Chapel. Jennifer was always busy. She was traveling to tournaments, going to school, and trying to find time to see her friends. But her parents knew they would have to decide soon whether or not to advise their daughter to become a professional. This was not an easy decision.

At the age of 12, Jennifer was winning tournaments and often beating girls much older. On the court she had the heart of a lion and was a fighter until the final point.

Tennis is one of the sports, along with swimming, where girls are ready to compete at an early age. There was a time when there was no age restriction on when a person could turn pro. But in 1986 the Women's International Professional Tennis Council ruled that girls had to be 14 years old before playing on the pro circuit. In 1990 the rule was modified so that a girl could begin professional play in the same month she turned 14.

Some people think the rule not allowing early pro competition was made because of two young tennis players—Tracy Austin and Andrea Jaeger. Both had begun playing at early ages and were very good. Austin won the 1977 national 18-and-under championship at 14, and later that year reached the quarter-finals of the U.S. Open. She won the U.S. Open two years later and again in 1981. For a brief period in 1980, she was ranked number one in the world.

Jaeger was just 4 feet 11 (150 centimeters) and weighed 78 pounds (35 kilograms) when she won the Orange Bowl 18-and-under title at age 13. In 1980, four months before her 15th birthday, she won her first pro tournament. Even though she never won a major championship, Jaeger was ranked as high as second for a while in 1981 and third in 1982. Both Tracy Austin and Andrea Jaeger each won well over a million dollars in prize money.

But both Austin and Jaeger saw their careers end early because of injuries. Austin suffered a series of back and neck injuries that began in 1983 when she was just 20 years old. Jaeger fell victim to arm and shoulder problems that began in 1984 when she was 19.

Many people thought that both girls had played too much tennis too soon. Perhaps their bodies were still growing and were not ready for the stress of big-time tennis. Ted Tinling, who had been part of the women's tennis scene for decades, said he thought that both practiced too much.

"Tracy, for instance, had a tight rotation on the backhand," said Tinling. "It wasn't fluid like Chris Evert's. That's what I feel led to her back problem. No one ever told her not to practice."

Austin admits that she sometimes pushed herself too hard. "It started when I damaged a sciatic nerve for the second time in 1982," she said. "I came back too soon then. In 1983 I had a stress fracture at Wimbledon," she said. "There were eight weeks until the U.S. Open, and I took off six. When I came back I played three hours a day and hurt my shoulder. The only thing I'd change if I did it over again would be to take it more slowly."

Jaeger also does not believe that simply too much tennis caused her problems. "I played five other sports," she said. "My exercise didn't come just

Tracy Austin was an intense young player who won a pair of U.S. Open titles before her 19th birthday. Yet just a short time later, recurring neck and back problems forced her into semi-retirement.

The athletic Andrea Jeager was the world's number-three player in both 1982 and 1983. Then came a shoulder injury in 1984 when she was just 19 years old; Jaeger was never a world-class player again.

from tennis. I'd play Nerf football for three hours, play soccer, and run.

"My shoulder problems started in South Africa in May 1984. I was playing night matches, and it was damp and cold. I could barely serve. After that, my arm was shot. It wasn't from practice. I can remember defaulting after winning a match at the Olympics in Los Angeles in 1984. My shoulder was so sore I couldn't even get my shirt off so the doctor could examine me."

Austin eventually became a tennis commentator. She admitted there was a big void in her life when she was forced to stop playing, but it eventually allowed her to develop in other ways. Jaeger said that it was "hard to walk by a court and not play. It's even hard to watch women's tennis on television. It's like a tease. You know you can still do it, but there's this line where you have to push yourself, and I can't."

Austin tried to come back as a doubles player only to be injured in a car accident. And Jaeger's shoulder will probably never be strong enough for her to play again.

The problems of these players were well known to the Capriati family as Jennifer continued to improve at the age of 13. In less than a year she could become a pro. And she was constantly being compared to Austin and Jaeger. Seena Hamilton, the director of the Easter Bowl, a junior tournament, spoke for many when she said, "Jennifer is without a doubt the most promising player since Tracy Austin and Andrea Jaeger."

The closer Jennifer came to turning pro, the more people compared her to Austin and Jaeger and expressed concerns about young women playing too much tennis. Stefano Capriati finally got tired of hearing it.

"What is the point of bringing them [Austin and Jaeger] up?" he asked. "They belong to the past. I believe in the future. Jennifer is a girl with a chance to be great."

Tracy Austin kept up on Jennifer's progress. She called her "exciting to watch," and added, "players like her come along once a decade." She warned Jennifer not to fall into the same traps she had.

"The biggest temptation is to overtrain," Austin said. "At Jennifer's age, you tend to see things short-term. She has to learn to take her time. If she gets hurt, she has to listen to her body instead of thinking, 'I've got to play Kansas City next week and Chicago the week after that.'"

Andrea Jaeger said there would be pressure on Jennifer. "If she gets hurt, people will say she started too young," Jaeger said. "If she throws a

After losing a tough point, Jennifer covers her face with her hands.

racket or swears or loses a lot of first-round matches, they'll say the pressure has gotten to her. Then she'll start thinking about the pressure, and the game won't be fun anymore."

The fun of playing the game was something that Austin believed would be crucial to Jennifer's success even after turning pro. "The most important thing is for her to enjoy tennis, even when she starts losing," Austin said. "She's got to develop her game and not be concerned with results. If she can, then the sky's the limit."

PRO DEBUT

From the beginning the Capriatis never gambled with Jennifer's physical condition. Her parents made sure that Jennifer's physical development was always carefully checked. They took her to a sports medicine clinic in Virginia when she was 12. They asked doctors to evaluate her development and suggest a series of exercises for her.

"We didn't go because she was sick or injured," said Mr. Capriati. "We went because she was healthy. The program she is using prevents injuries."

Most of the program involved a strict stretching routine, as well as massage to make sure muscles didn't tighten. Tight muscles could lead to pulls, strains, and other injuries. Mr. Capriati took care of the massage after each practice session. He also helped his daughter with some of the complex stretching exercises that the clinic advised. There were times when Jennifer wanted to stop before completing the stretches, but her father always insisted she finish.

The formula seemed to work. Jennifer was fit and ready to play. Fortunately Jennifer was getting bigger and stronger. As she approached her first pro tournament and her 14th birthday, she was 5 feet 6 (168 centimeters) and weighed almost 120 pounds (54 kilograms). The family finally announced that she would turn professional in March 1990. Her birthday was March 29, so she was eligible to play as a pro as soon as the month began. Her first pro event would be the Virginia Slims of Florida, scheduled for March 6 at The Polo Club in Boca Raton.

Jennifer prepared carefully. In November 1989 she played an exhibition match against 25-year-old Laura Gildemeister, a pro who was ranked among the top 25 in the world. Jennifer zipped through the match, 6-4, 6-1, giving a display of power tennis that surprised many onlookers. She didn't just return the ball to keep it in play. She hit every shot hard and aimed to win.

She even had the chance to hit with Martina Navratilova. Navratilova was Chris Evert's great rival over the years and was considered one of the best of all time. Jennifer and Navratilova didn't keep score, but Jennifer proved she could stay on the court with a legend.

"That was exciting," she said after the game. "I couldn't believe I was actually playing against Martina. She was really strong, much better than the people I usually play. She just has so many more things—more power, more shots, and a great serve."

The week before her professional debut was a busy one for Jennifer. It seemed as if everyone wanted an interview with her. Two conference calls were set up so she could talk to 30 reporters from the United States and England. ABC television did a segment on her at her home near

Interviews are a big part of the tennis life. Jennifer learned this from the moment she turned pro and has always been courteous and friendly when talking to the media.

Saddlebrook, and NBC taped a segment from there for the *Today* show. Neither network was allowed to film or tape her practice sessions.

Finally it was March 6, the day of her first professional match against Mary Lou Daniels. Now it was up to Capriati to play winning tennis. She proved herself, beating Daniels in straight sets. There was a great deal of publicity following her first win. But that was just the first match in the tournament, and Capriati couldn't afford to relax.

Besides playing singles, Capriati teamed with another all-time great, Billie Jean King, in doubles. King was 46 years old and enjoyed teaming with a partner not yet 14. The pair won their first-round match, much to the delight of another big crowd. They urged each other on, slapped hands with "high fives," and worked well together. Unfortunately, they were beaten in the second round. But Billie Jean King was impressed.

"It's really fun for me to see somebody her age and how well she handles things," King said.

Capriati's second-round singles match was against 21-year-old Claudia Porwik of West Germany, who was ranked 34th in the world. Once again Capriati experienced some highs and lows. She won the first set, 7-5. It was a tough battle and seemed to take some of the steam out of her. Porwik stormed back and won six straight games to take the second set, 6-0.

For the first time as a pro, Capriati had to show her character. She had said after her first match that she loved to fight, and she showed it here. She broke Porwik's serve twice in the third set and went on to win the match. It wouldn't get any easier. In her third match Capriati met Nathalie Tauziat of France. When someone said that Tauziat was ranked 16th in the world,

After a loss to Gabriela Sabatini, Jennifer is consoled by her father, Stefano.

Capriati showed her confidence by answering quickly, "It wouldn't matter if I were going against Steffi Graf."

Tauziat got off to a quick start and a 4-1 lead in the first set. Capriati turned it around. She won the next game without losing a point and took 11 of the next 13 games to win the match easily. When it ended, she blew a kiss to her father in the stands. She had now won her first three pro matches and would next face Helena Sukova, the world's 10th ranked player.

Many thought that the 6-foot-2 (188-centimeter) Sukova would have too much power for Capriati. But Capriati started the match with a service ace. It was clocked at 94 miles (148 kilometers) per hour, and Sukova didn't even touch it. From there, Capriati played some of her best tennis of the tournament, winning the set, 6-1. Sukova battled to a 4-3 lead in the second set. Then there was a rain delay, and when they started playing again it was Capriati all the way. She won 12 of the final 15 points to take the set, 6-4, and the match.

"I saw her hit yesterday and knew she was hitting the ball well, placing the ball well," Sukova said. "But I didn't think she could do it the whole match."

Capriati was certainly hitting well. Throughout the tournament she brought the crowd to its feet with hard-hit winners, spectacular returns, and big serves. In the semi-finals she defeated Laura Gildemeister, 7-6, 7-6, and won a pair of tiebreakers. In her very first tournament she had become the youngest player ever to reach the finals in women's play. But waiting for her was Gabriela Sabatini, the number-three ranked player in the world.

As good as Sabatini was, she still had a tough time with Capriati. Not once during the tournament did Capriati let the pressure overwhelm her. Even in the final she played well. Sabatini won, but the match was close. The final score was 6-4, 7-5. Capriati had surprised everyone.

"I had to play my best tennis to beat her," Sabatini said. "She should be at the top very soon."

ON THE PRO CIRCUIT

Capriati had impressed a lot of people in her first tournament. She was still a few weeks away from her 14th birthday, but she had already beaten

Being a tennis star doesn't mean you can't have fun. Here, Jennifer happily greets her fans in an outfit she would never wear on the court.

some of the top pros in the tennis world. Only good things were predicted for Jennifer Capriati.

"She can definitely be the leading person in the 1990s," said Pam Shriver, the 14th-ranked women's player in 1990.

"She was born to do this kind of work," said former pro Mary Carillo, who is now a TV tennis analyst. "And she's happy. That's her secret weapon."

Others pointed to the fact that the United States had not had a top women's player for some time. The current stars—Graf, Sanchez, Navratilova, Seles—were all Europeans. The United States was ready for a new tennis star. Chris Evert, who had dominated the scene for years, saw the same thing for Capriati.

"I think that everybody hopes so much that Jennifer is going to be the one," said Evert, "that she can be like Billie Jean and me, and can be number one in the world. Europe has been doing so well lately. It's as if we're starving for someone to come along and fill the void." Evert predicted that Capriati would crack the top ten by the end of the year.

Evert did have a point: The United States was the home of the majority of tournaments, but in 1990 did not have a young star to call its own. Evert had recently retired at age 35 after winning many championships. For a while it looked as if Austin and Jaeger would be the next great players. But injuries had stopped them early.

Along with Evert, Martina Navratilova had been a champion on the circuit for years. Navratilova was 33 years old in March 1990 and still a top performer. But Steffi Graf of Germany had taken over as the world's best player. In 1988 she had won the Grand Slam. That meant she won all four major tournaments: the Australian, French, and U.S. Opens, as well as Wimbledon. She also won the Olympic title that year.

Gabriela Sabatini of Argentina, Arantxa Sanchez of Spain, and Monica Seles, originally from Yugoslavia, were other young players vying for the top spot. This was the group that Capriati would try to join. Plans called for her to play in ten major tournaments during the next twelve months. It was a tough schedule.

Capriati tried to keep everything low key. "I think I'm just a kid. I have this talent, and I don't know why everyone is going crazy over it."

It seemed that youth was taking over the tennis world. In June, just two months after Capriati turned pro, Monica Seles had upset Graf to win the French Open. Seles was 16 years old. Graf was barely 21. Capriati played well in her first French Open. She battled her way into the semi-finals by beating Mary Joe Fernandez before losing to Seles. In spite of the loss, she became the youngest Grand Slam semi-finalist in history.

Capriati was proving she wasn't a flash in the pan. Although she still hadn't won any tournaments, she had won many matches, and she rose in the rankings. Like Chris Evert before her, Capriati used a two-hand back-hand stroke and could rally endlessly from the baseline. But she played more of a power game than Evert did and came to the net more often. Capriati had to play that way because power was her key to winning. Graf played a power game. Seles was getting more powerful. Sabatini and Sanchez could bang away for three sets.

Capriati continued to grow bigger and stronger. By the end of 1990 she was 5 feet 7 (170 centimeters) and weighed 135 pounds (61 kilograms). She

lost to Graf in the fourth round of the U.S. Open that year, but played a very tough match. She had also reached the finals of the Family Circle Cup where she lost to Navratilova. Shortly afterward she traveled to Puerto Rico and won her first tournament. The win qualified her for the Virginia Slims tournament at New York City's Madison Square Garden.

The Virginia Slims is the last big tournament of the tennis year. As luck would have it, Capriati drew Graf to play in the first round. It was a great match with both players slugging it out for three sets. When it ended, Graf had the victory, and Capriati was exhausted. However, she was now ranked number eight in the world, cracking the top ten as many had predicted she would.

It was a battle of teenagers at the 1990 French Open. Jennifer lost this match to Monica Seles, who would go on to win the championship.

She also earned some $300,000 in prize money her first year on the tour. Of course, she had already been paid many times that for endorsing tennis-related products, a fringe benefit that the most popular athletes today can count on.

Capriati continued to work hard to improve her game. As soon as there was a break in the schedule, she worked with weights to build her upper body strength. She also tried to develop a more powerful serve and worked on her footwork to become quicker at the net.

"I'm still not very comfortable at the net," she admitted at one point. "I don't think I'll ever really be a net person. I guess I was just born a baseliner. But still, I'm trying."

Her new coach, Tom Gullikson, himself a former pro, wanted her to play an all-around game. He felt she could be a dominant player.

"I definitely think Jennifer is beginning to play better," he said early in 1991. "Right now we're working on her intensity, her concentration, and her movement. We're also doing a lot of work with her serve. She should try to go out and play an entire match without losing her serve, the way the men do. Both Navratilova and Graf dominate matches with their first serves. There's no reason Jennifer shouldn't dominate, too."

CLOSER TO THE TOP

Capriati received a great deal of publicity her first year on the tour. She couldn't go anywhere in public without being recognized by admiring fans. People wanted to talk to her, get her autograph, and take her picture. Like many young athletes, she tried to do it all at first. She soon found that so much attention was difficult to handle.

"I love my fans, but I just can't be everything to everyone," she said. "People expect me to do all this stuff because I did it last year. But this year is a little different. Sometimes I need to be by myself and just be able to go and watch a match privately. I can't always sign autographs and talk to everyone."

This is a lesson all well-known athletes learn. It is part of being a star. And when you're barely 15 years old, it's even more difficult to handle. Capriati also expected more from herself on the court in 1991.

"Last year, playing good matches and getting close was enough," she said. "This year my goal is to forget about coming close and to beat some of these top players. I don't just want good matches. I want to win!"

Stefano Capriati continued to travel with his daughter, although his role had

At the U.S. Open championships in 1991, Capriati realized how popular she was. But she seemed to love her fans as much as they loved her, signing autographs and talking to them whenever she could.

changed somewhat. "Everybody wants her to give them time," he said. "But I know when enough is enough. So I'm now, as you say, 'the bad guy.' We learned the first year the importance of rest time. We didn't always manage time very well then. Jennifer had to realize she wasn't there for the press or for the people, but to play a tennis match. If you're tired or your mind is a little busy, it's not on tennis, and you can forget the reason you're there." In other words, he often had to make sure his daughter was left alone to rest, to stretch, and to do her homework.

Winning meant making sacrifices. Yet Jennifer tried to keep her life as normal as possible. She was now a ninth-grader at Saddlebrook's Palmer Academy, a private school. There were times when the older girls on the tour would help her with her homework and also times when she had to send her homework in by fax machine. Yet despite her hectic schedule, she continued to make the honor roll.

"She is an outstanding student," said school director Norman Palmer. "I wish all my students had her attitude."

The early part of the 1991 season saw Capriati beating the lesser players, but still having trouble with the top people. She lost to Helena Sukova at the Virginia Slims in Chicago. Then Sabatini beat her in the semi-final at Boca Raton, and Seles topped her in the quarter-finals of the Lipton tournament. With the French Open approaching, Capriati was feeling the pressure.

By 1991, after losing to a number of the top players, including Monica Seles at the Lipton Tournament, there was increasing pressure to win.

"I haven't really been thinking about my ranking," she said, "but I have thought, 'Uh oh, what if I don't get to the semis again in Paris?' People are probably expecting me to do all this stuff. That's part of tennis and you've got to learn how to deal with it. You've got to tell yourself that if you lose, it isn't the end of the world. You're doing it for yourself, and you can't worry about what other people think."

The big star of the 1991 season was Monica Seles. Now 5 feet 9 (175 centimeters) and 120 pounds (54 kilograms), Seles had developed a two-fisted power attack that would help her win three of the four Grand Slam events. (She didn't play Wimbledon due to a minor injury.) Only 17 years old and already number one in the world, Seles seemed to know that in the coming seasons her toughest opponent would be Jennifer Capriati, who is younger than she by two years.

"When Graf was number one, she knew probably that Sabatini and I would be giving her the toughest competition," said Seles. "Now I know that Capriati will be there. She's not a one-week player or anything like that. She's here to stay, and she'll be a tough opponent for many, many years to come."

Seles also thought Capriati would soon crack the top five in the rankings. Capriati didn't make the semis in Paris, but at Wimbledon later in the summer she played very well. She quickly showed that grass courts

Here Capriati has just beaten Martina Navratilova in a quarter-final match at Wimbledon in 1991, by a score of 6-4, 7-5.

didn't bother her. Her enthusiasm and powerful play had the British fans rooting for her.

In the quarter-finals, Capriati went up against Navratilova, a player whom she had not beaten in eleven previous matches. In the first set Capriati slugged it out with the veteran and came away with a 6-4 victory. But in the second set Navratilova began to come back. She had a 3-2 lead with a service break when the match was interrupted by rain.

During the overnight delay, Stefano Capriati gave his daughter some advice. "Just go out and enjoy," he told her. "Play. Have fun."

Capriati was loose and relaxed the next day when the match resumed. With the second set tied at 5-5, Navratilova had eight break points on Capriati's serve. Capriati fought like a tiger and won each of the key points. On the last point, Capriati threw up a perfect backhand lob as Navratilova charged the net. The ball landed in bounds, and Navratilova turned to her opponent and applauded along with everyone else. Capriati held serve to go ahead at 6-5, then broke Navratilova's serve to win the set, 7-5, and the match. She had finally beaten the great Martina.

Capriati was now the youngest semi-finalist in Wimbledon history. She was 15 years old. Once again she had to face Gabriela Sabatini. Someone asked Denise Capriati about the possibility of her daughter winning the whole tournament. Mrs. Capriati replied, "You know, part of me doesn't want this to happen yet."

Mrs. Capriati knew the kind of pressure and attention that would go with winning Wimbledon. Many tennis fans think that Wimbledon is the most prestigious tournament in the world. The match with Sabatini was hard-fought and close. But Sabatini had a better day and won it, 6-4, 6-4. Still Capriati put on a great show. The crowds loved her. In the eyes of most experts and the other players, she was getting closer to the top.

PROVING HERSELF

In the weeks following Wimbledon, Capriati continued to play well. Whenever she played she had an intense, determined look on her face. When someone asked how she had changed since turning pro little more than a year earlier, Capriati gave a surprising answer. She said she was meaner.

"On the tennis court I can't be nice," was the way she put it. "I say to myself, 'Come on, you don't want to lose. Fight back.' And I like fighting."

"I like fighting" was something she had said earlier in her career. That spirit was even more a part of her now. She knew how hard she had to play against the top pros. Soon it began to come together. In early August she was in Carlsbad, California, for the Mazda Classic. Sure enough, the final came down to a Capriati-Seles match. The stadium was packed to watch the two teenagers compete.

It was a strange match. Seles took the opening set, 6-4, seeming to have an advantage with her power game. But in the second set, Capriati stormed back. She was all over the court with an awesome display of quickness and power. She won the set easily, 6-1. So the two came out for a third and final set.

This became another war, both players slugging from the baseline. With the set tied at 6-6, it went to a tiebreaker, and Capriati won. Not only had she finally triumphed over Monica Seles, but she took home the largest purse of her career—$100,000.

A week later she was in Toronto, Canada, for the Player's Challenge. In the final she topped Katerina Maleeva, 6-2, 6-3, for another victory. "I'm on top; I'm there now," she said, excitedly after the victory. She was ranked seventh in the world now, and many felt she had a good chance to win the upcoming U.S. Open.

Whether she won or lost the Open, it would still be a good year for Capriati. It was estimated that she would win nearly $600,000 in prize money. But her endorsement money was going to come in at $4.5 million, placing her fourth in

The toughest part of being a pro at 14 is finding time to be a kid. At the Lipton tournament in 1990, Jennifer managed to spend time with her brother and one of her friends from home.

earnings among all women tennis players. She was also 26th on the *Forbes* magazine list of the world's highest-paid athletes.

Even with that kind of achievement, Capriati wasn't spoiled. Whenever she went home to Saddlebrook, she would look up her old friends and spend the day with them. They would go to the movies or a shopping mall and just have fun. It was a welcome break from the pressures of the professional tennis tour.

Capriati spent her money carefully. Although she was learning to drive at the end of 1991, she hadn't bought a car. Instead, she loved buying cassette tapes. Her musical tastes were varied. She liked rap, mellow rock, and classical music. One expensive gift she did buy was a diamond tennis bracelet for her mother's birthday.

"Everyone thinks we go shopping and buy all kinds of stuff," Denise Capriati said. "When we go shopping, Jennifer will try something on, but she'll usually say, 'Do I really need this?' or 'I don't really have to have that.' She's still pretty practical."

The U.S. Open came around again in September 1991, and Capriati's hopes were high. It was only her second Open, but a lot was expected of Capriati. Even though she was just 15, people now thought of her as one of the best. And they were right. She proved it in the early rounds, winning her matches easily. Sure enough, she stormed into the semi-finals, and waiting for her once more was Monica Seles.

Both girls were playing very well, and their match promised to be an exciting one. It turned out to be more than that. Among other things it was called "the single most extraordinary match ever between two players—male or female—under the age of 18."

Both Capriati and Seles were on top of their games. Most of the match was played from the baseline. The pace and accuracy of their ground strokes were nothing short of amazing. Each player seemed to hit all out at each stroke of every rally. Seles grunted loudly with each shot she made, and Capriati was also vocal during the heat of battle.

The crowd became very involved in the match. Seles won the first set, 6-3, and seemed to be in charge despite Capriati's aggressive play. Then in the second set their roles reversed. Capriati was the sharper of the two, and she won the set, 6-3. After two sets, they were dead even. For nearly the entire third set, neither player gave an inch.

Both players chased down every ball. Each made a number of nearly impossible shots. Finally the third set was tied at 6 games each. The entire match came down to a seven-point tiebreaker. At 2-2, Seles double-faulted to allow Capriati a 3-2 lead. Capriati was just four points from reaching the final. Then Seles showed what a great player she was. She somehow raised her game just a notch and won the final five points, taking the tiebreaker, 7-3, and the final set, 7-6, to win the match.

"Seles prevailed because she had a bit more courage and will to survive," was the way one reporter put it.

But neither lacked courage. Both of these young women had played their hearts out. Seles returned to defeat Navratilova for the title, and Capriati had won more respect from her peers and from tennis fans the world over.

The Capriati-Seles rivalry would continue for years to come. There was no doubt that Capriati was now among the top women players in the world. She had beaten all the top women pros except Steffi Graf. However, by May

1992 she still had not won any additional tournaments. She was ranked sixth in the world, her highest ranking yet.

Yet as she turned 16 years old there were still questions. Would the competitive fires continue to burn? Would she continue to put in the hours and the work to climb that final mountain? Until a player won Grand Slam events, she wasn't considered truly great. So the pressure to win the French, Australian, and U.S. Open tournaments, and Wimbledon, continued to mount.

When Capriati first joined the pro tour at 14, her mother tried to look at both sides. "At first, I didn't want her to do the tour because I thought it might be too much," she said. "But it gave her the opportunity to make friends, and it gave the other girls the chance to see that she's just a normal kid doing the same things that they're doing, except that she's a little younger."

Jennifer Capriati would not always be the young challenger. One day, other teenagers would join the tour, and Capriati would be one of the veterans. At the age of 15, whether she became a champion and followed in the footsteps of her early idol, Chris Evert, remained to be seen. No one ever doubted that she had the talent. She also had help and guidance, a caring family, and good friends.

The rest would be up to her.

At the 1991 U.S. Open, Jennifer was intense between points, pumping her fist to remind herself to keep playing hard. She wound up losing to Seles in a very close semi-final, but it was one of the best matches ever played.

JENNIFER CAPRIATI: HIGHLIGHTS

1976   Born on March 29 in New York, New York.

1979   Picks up tennis racket for the first time at age 3.

1980   Moves to Lauderhill, Florida, to study with Jimmy Evert.

1986   Moves to Wesley Chapel, Florida, to train at the Saddlebrook
            International Tennis Center.

1988   Becomes the youngest ever to win both the national 18-and-under clay-
            court championship and the 18-and-under hard-court title.
            Wins the junior championships at the French and U.S. Open tournaments.

1990   Makes professional debut at Virginia Slims of Florida tournament
            and becomes the youngest player ever to reach the finals in women's
            play.
            Plays in the French Open and becomes the youngest Grand Slam semi-
            finalist in history.
            Plays in the U.S. Open for the first time, losing to Steffi Graf in the
            fourth round.
            Reaches the finals of the Family Circle Cup.
            Wins her first professional tournament in Puerto Rico.
            Ranked number eight in the world, after losing to Steffi Graf at the
            Virginia Slims tournament in New York.

1991   Becomes the youngest semi-finalist in Wimbledon history.
            Wins the Mazda Classic, beating Monica Seles in the finals.
            Wins the Players' Challenge in Toronto, beating Katerina Maleeva.
            Reaches the semi-finals in the U.S. Open, losing the final tiebreaker
            to Monica Seles.
            Ranked sixth in the world.

1992   Wins Olympic Gold Metal in Barcelona, beating Steffi Graf.
            Wins the Mazda Classic, beating Conchita Martinez in the finals.

FIND OUT MORE

Aaseng, Nathan. *Winning Women of Tennis*. Minneapolis, Minn.: Lerner, 1981.

Gutman, Bill. *Go For It: Tennis*. Lakeville, Conn.: Grey Castle Press, 1989.

Smith, Stan and Tom Valentine. *Inside Tennis*. Chicago: Contemporary Books, 1974.

Books on other women tennis stars:

Leder, Jane M. *Martina Navratilova*. New York: Puffin Books, 1989.

Monroe, Judy. *Steffi Graf*. New York: Macmillan, 1988.

Porter, A.P. *Zina Garrison*, Minneapolis, Minn.: Lerner, 1992.

How to write to Jennifer Capriati:

Jennifer Capriati
c/o IMG
One Erieview Plaza
Cleveland, Ohio 44114

INDEX